Author:
John Malam studied ancient history and archeology at the University of Birmingham, England, after which he worked as an archeologist at the Ironbridge Gorge Museum in Shropshire. He is now an author, specializing in nonfiction books for children. He lives in Cheshire, England, with his wife and their two children.

Artist:
David Antram was born in Brighton, England, in 1958. He studied at Eastbourne College of Art and then worked in advertising for 15 years before becoming a full-time artist. He has illustrated many children's nonfiction books.

Series creator:
David Salariya was born in Dundee, Scotland. He has illustrated a wide range of books and has created and designed many new series for publishers in the UK and overseas. David established The Salariya Book Company in 1989. He lives in Brighton with his wife, illustrator Shirley Willis, and their son, Jonathan.

Editor: **Victoria England**

Editorial Assistant: **Mark Williams**

© The Salariya Book Company Ltd MMXII

No part of this publication may be reproduced in whole or in part, or stored in a retrieval system, or transmitted in any form or by any means, electronic, mechanical, photocopying, recording, or otherwise, without written permission of the publisher. For information regarding permission, write to the copyright holder.

Published in Great Britain in 2012 by
The Salariya Book Company Ltd
25 Marlborough Place, Brighton BN1 1UB

ISBN-13: 978-0-531-20873-1 (lib. bdg.)   978-0-531-20948-6 (pbk.)
ISBN-10: 0-531-20873-7 (lib. bdg.)   0-531-20948-2 (pbk.)

All rights reserved.
Published in 2012 in the United States
by Franklin Watts
An imprint of Scholastic Inc.
Published simultaneously in Canada.

A CIP catalog record for this book is available
from the Library of Congress.

Printed and bound in China.
Printed on paper from sustainable sources.
1 2 3 4 5 6 7 8 9 10 R 21 20 19 18 17 16 15 14 13 12

SCHOLASTIC, FRANKLIN WATTS, and associated logos are trademarks and/or registered trademarks of Scholastic Inc.

PAPER FROM
SUSTAINABLE
FORESTS

uldn't Want to Be a
Ninja Warrior!

Written by
John Malam

Illustrated by
David Antram

Created and designed by
David Salariya

A Secret Job That's Your Destiny

Franklin Watts®
An Imprint of Scholastic Inc.
NEW YORK • TORONTO • LONDON • AUCKLAND • SYDNEY
MEXICO CITY • NEW DELHI • HONG KONG
DANBURY, CONNECTICUT

Contents

Introduction

Do you have what it takes to be a ninja warrior? Could you make it as one of Japan's silent, stealthy, and fearsome fighters? First, you need to know what life is like for a "shadow warrior"— then maybe you'll decide you wouldn't want to be a ninja at all!

It's around the year 1550, and Japan is at war with itself. Future historians will call it the Warring States Period. For you, that means you're on active service for a warlord. He's the most powerful man in your state, and you must do whatever he orders you to do. He's sure a rival warlord is about to attack.

NINJA is a Japanese word written as two characters. The top character means *nin* ("to do quietly") and the lower one means *ja* ("person").

HOWEVER IMPOSSIBLE the challenge, you must keep your nerve and serve your lord and master to the very end.

Feudal Japan

EMPEROR. The ultimate leader, but he is a figurehead and rules without power.

SHOGUN. A military dictator who is Japan's real leader with unlimited power.

DAIMYO. A warlord and head of a clan who rules one of Japan's many states.

SAMURAI. A warrior and member of the upper class in Japanese society.

PEASANTS. The vast majority of working people who belong to the lower class.

State Wars! Japan's

In the sixteenth century, Japan is divided into many small states or kingdoms, each of which is ruled by a *daimyo*. He is a warlord and ruler of the state. Japan's states are almost always at war with each other. To protect their territory from rivals, each warlord has his own army.

Age of Battles

As fighting has increased, these armies have become larger and more organized. The most powerful warlords have forces of more than 100,000 men. This is a time of civil war. It is an age of battles when rival states are attacking each other, trying to win territory. As a ninja warrior, you must play your part in history.

Handy Hint

Battlefields are full of flags of family emblems (*mon*)—that's how soldiers recognize their own side.

I need to get my eyes tested!

Ninjas! Men (and Women) in Black

The ninja warriors of Japan have been around for a long time. These secretive men—and sometimes women—take great care to disguise their identities, pretending to be farmers or other members of the peasantry. When called upon, they work for warlords as spies, secret agents, saboteurs, and assassins. These are the skills of *ninjutsu*—the art of stealth. These people will stop at nothing to complete a mission, and for this reason they are both despised and feared. They are the lowest of the low in society, and you will be one of them!

Some say I am a shadow— an invisible warrior.

Handy Hint

If you become a ninja, you'll want to keep your identity a secret, so disguise yourself as a peasant.

Ninja Origins

AN OLD STORY says ninjas are descended from the *tengu*—terrifying long-nosed, half-man, half-crow demons.

IN TRUTH, ninjas may have come to Japan from China in the AD 900s, when warriors fled that land in search of safety.

THE GREATEST AREA of ninja concentration is in the provinces of Iga and Kaga in central Japan.

Kaga

Iga

9

Destiny! Born to Be a Ninja

A ninja is born, not made. From the moment you are born your whole life is planned out for you. You are the son—or daughter—of a ninja. Your family can trace its roots back through many generations of ninjas, and each one of them has lived to serve a warlord.

You live in a ninja village in the mountains. It's so remote that outsiders think it's just a legend, an imaginary place. It looks like an ordinary farming village, but you know this is only a disguise to keep your secret safe. From an early age, you have been trained by your father in the craft of ninjutsu—passing on the skills he knows to equip you for your life as a ninja.

Don't think of them as bamboo canes—imagine they're enemy fighters!

First Lessons in Ninjutsu

Don't knock me off!

AGE 5: BALANCE. You walk along a narrow beam to improve your balance.

10

Handy Hint

Listen to your father! He has lots of good advice about your training.

Mmmmmm

AGE 5: AGILITY. You leap over bushes to improve how well and quickly you can move your body.

AGE 9: FLEXIBILITY. You practice movements that will make your joints flexible so you can stretch your body without injury.

AGE 11: KICKING. You practice kicking techniques against bundles of straw.

AGE 12: SELF-DEFENSE. You learn how to use a wooden staff to protect yourself.

Get Dressed! Your Ninja Costume

At about the age of 15 you will start to work, dress, and be regarded as an adult. You will wear the clothes of a peasant farmer and work in the village fields, tending to crops and animals. Tidy hair is important for Japanese of all ranks—messy hair is considered a disgrace. If you're a man, yours will be pulled back and tied in a bun, and the sides of your head will be shaved. If strangers do come to your village, all they will see is a hardworking, tidy young man and his proud father.

Do I have to muck out the animals' stalls today, Dad?

Someone has to do it!

But you know the truth. At home, tucked out of sight of prying eyes, are your ninja clothes. When you put them on you are transformed from an ordinary peasant into an extraordinary "man in black." All who see you now will fear and respect you.

This is more like it!

MASK
Covers head and face; only eyes are visible.

SHIRT
Worn under jacket; has tight arms.

Handy Hint
When you're not wearing them, keep your ninja clothes out of sight to protect your identity.

That's my boy!

1. 2. 3.

How to Wear Your Mask

1. TOP CLOTH. Cover the top of your head with a cloth. Tie it in a knot at the back of your head.
2. LOWER CLOTH. Cover your lower face with another cloth. Tie it in a knot at the back of your head. Make sure this knot is on top of the first knot.
3. THIRD KNOT. Knot the top cloth again—this time on top of the lower cloth knot. The cloths will not fall off, no matter how much you move.

BELT
Long; wrapped around waist several times.

BAG
Hangs at waist; holds small tools and equipment.

JACKET
Loose fit.

PANTS
Tied at knees.

GAITERS
Worn over calves.

SOCKS
With separate section for big toe.

SANDALS
Made of straw.

CHAIN MAIL ARMOR. It's heavy and it's uncomfortable, but this shirt of iron could save your life. Wear it under your jacket.

13

Ninja School! Ninja Organization

Ninjas are very well organized. You belong to a school or group known as a *ryu*. The leader of the school is the commander in chief, known as a *jonin* (headman). He takes orders from the *daimyo*—the warlord in charge of the state. The jonin is a wise man, and he decides whether or not to send his ninjas into action.

The jonin keeps his identity secret by using couriers to carry messages for him. He sends messages to *chunin,* or middlemen, and they use couriers to communicate with the *genin,* or low men. The genin are the ninjas who will carry out the warlord's orders.

Daimyo (warlord)

Courier

I know who to send!

Get me those attack plans!

Jonin (headman)

14

Who's Who

DAIMYO. *Warlord in charge of the state overall. Gives orders to the jonin.*

Handy Hint

Don't ask questions—if the jonin wanted you to know who he is, he'd tell you. Curiosity will get you in trouble!

COURIER. *A messenger who delivers messages between the members of the ninja school.*

JONIN. *Headman of the ryu. Takes orders from the daimyo and passes them to the chunin.*

CHUNIN. *Middleman of the ninja school. Takes orders from the jonin and passes them to the genin.*

GENIN. *The low men of the ninja school— the ninjas themselves.*

I know who to send!

Chunin (middleman)

Courier

Genin (ninja— that's you!)

Why me?

Weapons! Ninja Tool Kit

Shuriken (throwing star)

You will learn how to use the weapons of a ninja. There are many to choose from, so pay close attention to your father as he teaches you how to master the skills of the sword, the staff, and the throwing stars. Each one is a formidable weapon. If you do badly in your lessons you will be a disappointment to yourself, your family, and your warlord master. If you are a lazy student, or don't practice with your weapons every day, you will be giving your enemy an advantage.

Ninjato (sword)

Sword

The sword is your main weapon. First you must draw the blade from its scabbard with lightning speed. Then, you must practice the correct two-handed grip before learning how to cut and slash with the razor-sharp steel blade.

Saya (scabbard)

On your way, my little star!

Handy Hint

For best results, learn to make smooth, flowing body movements with your staff. Don't stand still with it!

Throwing Stars

With sharp edges and piercing points, throwing stars are like swords hidden in the hand. Learn to throw them at your foe, or hold them tight for hand-to-hand combat.

Staff

Stick-fighting skills are essential for every ninja. You will train with the short, medium, and long staffs, learning when and how to use them. Master the skills of *bojutsu*—staff fighting—and your enemy is sure to be the loser.

Bo (staff)

17

Hidden! Make Yourself Invisible

f all the skills you will learn, the craft of invisibility is the most cunning. It will teach you how to hide from your enemies, tricking them into thinking you are not there. Dressed in black, no one will see you coming, and as you stealth walk toward them with "phantom steps" you will be in total control. But if you disturb animals, causing them to make sudden movements, or if you tread on twigs, making them snap, the silence will be broken and your cloak of invisibility will slip. Your enemies will sense your presence, and you will have to act fast to avoid attack.

> Sssh! People are trying to sleep!

Stealth Walk Like a Ninja

1. Small step. For moving through shallow waters or leaves.
2. Sideways walking. For moving through shadows and passageways.
3. Sweeping step. For moving over planks or matting.

1.   *2.*   *3.*

4. Turning step. For moving across open spaces.
5. Cross step. For moving during the night.

4.   *5.*

How to Disappear

ON YOUR KNEES: Crawl through long grass on your hands and knees.

UNDERWATER: Breathe through a hollow bamboo cane.

Oops!

ON YOUR BELLY: Crawl on your belly for an ultralow profile.

LOOK, NO HANDS! Black half-gloves will hide the exposed skin of your hands.

CLIMB: Scale up the underside of a staircase.

SMOKE BOMB: Throw a smoke bomb and vanish into its thick smoke.

Crack!

19

Mission!
You Have Your Orders

Your training is over. Are you ready to be called a ninja warrior? The jonin has received word that your state is about to be attacked by a rival warlord, and the chunin now has to pick a group of ninjas for a dangerous mission. They have to break into the castle of the enemy warlord and steal his plans for the upcoming attack. If the chunin picks you, you must accept. To succeed, you will have to prepare yourself, both physically and mentally.

I'm not sure I'm ready for this!

Equipment You Will Need:

1. Grappling hook. For climbing and swinging.
2. Tiger claws. For attacking an enemy and climbing walls and trees.
3. Climbing hook. Fits into cracks in walls.
4. Device for listening to conversations through walls.

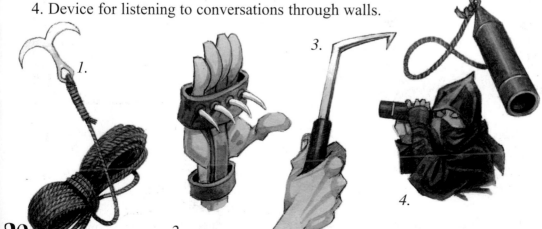

1.

2.

3.

4.

Prepare Your Body

You must be in superior health and in the right state of mind if you are to succeed. Preparation is the key to ninja success, and although your father has taught you all he knows, there are some things you have to do for yourself.

This is what you are to do...

Handy Hint
Write a spell for protection. Hang it on your wall and also carry it with you.

I'm so bored!

PATIENCE. Spend days alone in a small room—it will improve your patience.

WARRIOR FOOD. White rice is easier to digest than brown rice. White is also the color of victory. Soybeans are the "warrior's food" or "magic food."

NIGHT OWL. Stay awake all night. This will help you get used to working in the dark.

ENDURANCE. Hang upside down from a tree for hours at a time. This will test how well you cope with difficult situations.

SWIM. Go for long swims. This will improve your strength and your ability to stay alert for long periods of time.

21

Break In! Enter the Enemy Castle

You have reached the great stone castle of the warlord, and somewhere inside are the plans you have come to steal. The first challenge will be to break through the castle's outer defenses. When you reach the keep, you must climb its high wall using grappling hooks, rope ladders, and your own body strength. If you are well prepared, you will have no fear of heights. But if your mind is weak, don't think about the emptiness beneath your feet or you may be paralyzed with fear, unable to climb any higher. This is not the time to lose your nerve!

It's scary! I can't see the bottom!

Teamwork

You must work as part of the ninja team, supporting your comrades no matter what dangers you face. Scaling the castle wall is just the beginning of the mission—who knows what you will find once you are inside!

22

SHIELD OF STONE.
The central keep is where the warlord lives. If you break through the outer defenses, his men will try to trap you in a courtyard, where you will be easy to attack.

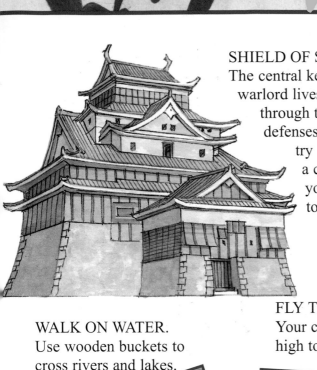

Handy Hint

Don't forget to take a *shikoro*— a thin saw— to cut through the wooden bars of a window.

WALK ON WATER.
Use wooden buckets to cross rivers and lakes.

FLY THROUGH THE AIR.
Your comrades will throw you high to "fly" you over walls.

LEAP OVER GAPS. Use a pole to vault over gaps.

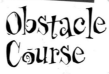

Obstacle Course

Walls, rivers, and wide gaps are some of the obstacles you must get past.

CLIMB A ROPE.
Hold on tight!

CLIMB A ROPE LADDER.
Use this instead of a rope.

WINDOW. A wooden window is the castle's weak point.

23

Found! The Enemy's Secret Plans

The castle is a massive building with courtyards, passageways, and rooms. You move quickly and silently, remembering to walk with phantom steps. To cross the wide-open spaces of courtyards, you use the ninja's turning step, scanning all around for signs of danger. In darkened, narrow passages you use sideways walking, your back to the wall and your sword held out in front of you. The longer you spend here, the greater your risk of being discovered.

At last you find what you are looking for—the enemy warlord's plans. As you pack the scrolls into a bag, you see a guard coming toward you. It's too late to hide! He raises the alarm, and now you are in terrible danger. Will your skills of ninjutsu save you from what is about to happen?

Ways to Divert Attention

DISTRACTION. Throw a pebble onto a roof—it will make a noise and guards will come to investigate.

24

Handy Hint

Metal spikes called caltrops will slow down pursuers who step on them as they come after you.

HELP!

HORSES. Open the stable doors and let the horses out.

SMALL FIRES. Start a fire inside a building—it will spread quickly.

ARSENAL. Go into the weapons store and break the enemy's spears.

Attacked! The Enemy Finds You

lerted by the sound of the alarm, the warlord's men are suddenly all around you. Swords are drawn, smoke bombs explode, and throwing stars fly toward their targets. You are outnumbered. Arrows streak silently toward you, and the ear-splitting crack of a firearm tells you the enemy is using muskets—a deadly new weapon. Look for an escape route over the wall. Whatever you do, do not lose the warlord's attack plans!

Spare me!

What was that?

Know Your Enemy

WARLORD. He's the daimyo or clan leader. As the most powerful man in the state, he has thousands of soldiers in his army.

Handy Hint

Blow powder into an attacker's eyes—it'll blind him just long enough for you to escape.

Leave him! Time to go!

FOOT SOLDIER. He's the backbone of the warlord's army. In his hand is a naginata—a curved blade on a long pole.

ARQUEBUSIER. He uses the arquebus, a new weapon that shoots a ball of solid lead.

ARCHER. The arrows fired from his longbow can go through metal chain mail.

Smoke bombs create clouds of thick smoke—the enemy won't be able to see you. Flash bombs make a bright flash, blinding the enemy for a few seconds. Firecrackers are loud and jump around on the ground, causing the enemy to panic.

Escape! Back to Safety

The smoke screen has worked, and you make your escape. Over the wall you go, keeping the warlord's attack plans close to you. It's a long way to the ground, but it doesn't seem to take any time at all to rappel down the rope. You wait for the rest of the team to join you, and then you begin the long journey home. The enemy has orders to recover the plans at all costs, but your ninja skills of stealth and invisibility will protect you until you reach the safety of your own land.

When you are home, go straight to the chunin and hand him the enemy's plans. Only then can you settle back into your everyday routine of constant training—until you're called on once again to serve your master.

So far, so good!

Mission Complete

ATTACK PLANS. The chunin will pass the enemy plans to the jonin, and he will pass them to the daimyo.

PROUD FATHER. Your father will be pleased to see you— you have made him a proud man.

BACK TO TRAINING. Practice your ninjutsu skills. You never know which ones you will need.

THE FUTURE. You are young and have a long life ahead and many missions to look forward to.

Handy Hint

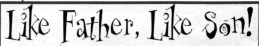

If your escape rope is too short to reach the ground, take off your clothes and tie them together, then tie them to the rope.

Like Father, Like Son!

PASS IT ON. One day, if you have children of your own, you will teach them the craft of ninjutsu, just as your father taught you. This is how the way of the warrior will be passed on to the next generation.

Glossary

Arquebus A type of musket (long-barreled gun) introduced into Japan in the 1540s. The Japanese called it a *teppo*.

Arsenal A store of weapons.

Bo Japanese word for "staff."

Bojutsu The art of stick fighting using a staff.

Caltrop A small metal spike that stands on the ground, pointing upward; used against foot soldiers and horses.

Chain mail Armor made of small metal rings linked together.

Chunin A ninja officer who acted as a middleman.

Courier A messenger.

Daimyo A warlord and ruler of a state or territory.

Emperor The head of state. As a figurehead ruler he had no power to make laws or command the people.

Feudal system A system of society in which the rich owned the land, and the poor worked on the land for the rich landowners.

Gaiters A cloth covering that runs from the knee to the ankle.

Genin Ordinary ninjas. It means "low men."

Grappling hook A hook at the end of a rope.

Jonin A ninja officer who was the headman of the group.

Keep The central tower of a castle.

Mon A family, clan, or religious symbol on a flag.

Musket A long-barreled gun that fires a ball of lead.

Naginata A curved blade at the end of a long pole.

Ninja A secret agent, spy, saboteur, or assassin. Ninjas had very low status in

Japanese society. The name means "a person who does things quietly."

Ninjato A sword used by a ninja.

Ninjutsu The skills used by a ninja.

Phantom steps A silent, secretive way of moving.

Rappel To descend from a high place using a rope lowered to the ground.

Ryu A group or school of ninjas.

Saboteur A person who deliberately disrupts or destroys something, especially by secret means.

Samurai A warrior from the upper classes of Japanese society.

Saya The scabbard for a ninja sword.

Shikoro A thin, foldaway saw.

Shogun Commander of the forces or general. A military dictator with unlimited power; the true ruler of feudal Japan.

Shuriken A small metal blade, sometimes shaped like a star, thrown at an enemy.

Staff A stick weapon that varied in length from short to long.

Stealth A silent, secretive way of moving or behaving.

Stealth walk A way of walking used by ninjas to avoid detection.

Warlord A powerful military commander in charge of a state.

Warring States Period The period from 1467 to 1600 in Japanese history, when the country's feudal states were at war with each other.

Index